In the Light of Peace

Birdbath, Lorenzo Valensi

In the Light of Peace

Edited by Leiah Bowden

with Abby Bogomolny, Sally Churgel, and Rita Rapoport Rowan

Bayit: Building Jewish • 2021

ISBN 978-0-578-85602-5

Permissions and previous publication information
appear on page 123; copyrights for the individual poems
in this collection are held by their authors.

Cover artwork: "Cherub," by Leiah Bowden.

For inquiries: Bayit: Building Jewish
9 Windflower Way
Williamstown MA 01267
www.yourbayit.org

Learn more about Congregation Ner Shalom at
www.nershalom.org

To the Jews of Sobeslav, Czech Republic,
lost in the Shoah
to whom we are deeply indebted
for the guardianship of their Torah scroll.
We carry their unsung poetry
in our hearts and our prayers.

Contents

Time and Seasons

Relationships

Praise

Openings

Introduction

An'im z'mirot v'shirim e'erog
Ki eylekha nafshi ta'arog.

I paint melodies and weave songs
For my soul longs for You…

So opens the medieval Jewish hymn *Shir Hakavod*, nailing
in just a few words the how and why of poetry. The how?
Pour out beauty! Weave words and images! (Usually easier
said than done.) And the why? Because our longing is
fairly bursting out of us: longing for God, for love, for past
or future, for the dead, for a second chance. We write
because this yearning doesn't allow us to be silent, or our
pens to be still.

This is the deep ache that is present in all the poems in this
book, each in its own elegant form.

Congregation Ner Shalom, in the heart of Sonoma County,
California, is a community disproportionately peopled
with musicians, writers, and artists among its many
spiritual seekers. How so many skilled weavers of words
found their way into a single community at a shared
moment of time is a mystery I cannot hope to solve. But I
am grateful to be here to witness and be part of it. The
words of the Ner Shalomers who contributed to *In The
Light of Peace* have excited, inspired, and soothed us in hard
times. And they continue to bring us to profound places.

I hope some of these poems are useful for you as prayer or
meditation or rallying cry. And I hope all of these poems
serve as an invitation to your own holy longing.

Rabbi Irwin Keller
Spiritual Leader
Congregation Ner Shalom
Sonoma County, California

In the Light of Peace

Reflection

הנני

Clouds in Hudson River Granite, Leiah Bowden

A Six-Word Short Story

Nancy Rapp

Shawl of snow.
Homesick.
Hot soup.

The Lighted Pull of Dreams

Abby Lynn Bogomolny

inky black of moonlit sea
our walk at midnight
by the lighthouse

warm in bundles from the cold
after a day of rain and dimness
in housebound January

at night i fly over the hill
        where mist lingers
in silver patches

    breathe
    the airbourne fog

a fringe of redwood fingers
  brushes my gleaming torso

outstretched wings glide me
i am pulled by the sureness of
of gravity
and my love
of returning to you

with the turning
earth, so do we
half in waking, the other half,
sleep
we fall inside, unwind
and retreat

as green things twist
an inch
by inch daily
towards the sun,
we drift closer
to the lighted pull of dreams

invisible to eyes outside
we fall, fill ourselves and fly

flapping and feeding
we flock like seagulls
to the lighted pull of dreams

Hope

Alexandra Ellen Appel

comes in such a small package
I had to look twice to recognize her
"You've been away so long," I said, "where ya' been?"

Silence, but then, what did I expect
a dissertation on desertion abandonment death?
hope is impossible small spoiled

expectation without evidence she arrives
again, with hope
such a small package
impossible to recognize, the tiny miracles
fleeting chance momentary grace,

the crash of the surf against the shore
the screech of a gull.

Remains

Alexandra Ellen Appel

deep beneath the green shoots
and roots in an early spring
look beyond the rock

and ice of past regrets and heartache
seek the questions
begging to be written in the book of night,

the answers that never come,
remain until the sun does set
and rises again every day as it must

offering hope
for life to continue
even when the tide washes us away

our bodies forgotten
there we remain
in the shoots

and roots of an early spring
begging to be remembered
for a past we did not invent
and the regrets that changed our lives
as we searched the answers

this is a way of aging
when what remains is less than what was
and understanding nothing is as it seems

only imagined as if some other way was the way
and breathing in the now the only breath to take
dig deep, dig long
find the shoots and roots of early spring
in the deep cavern of what is gone before.

Promises

Basha

scattered about my doorway like September
leaves I crush them as I go inside
their crumbs sometimes stumble into
the living room and I must sweep them up
to keep the entrance clean.

I wish I could stack them, as I do
the magazines I vow to read on winter evenings
or that I could complete in dreams
the wishes laid beside my bed.

The edges of the pages curl with time
like the book left on the porch bench that
was caught by morning mist
now for ever wrinkled but not really read.

I sometimes leave the cupboards
open thinking I will come back to
finish sorting grains from nuts
to line up every type of vinegar
with special spices
expecting to create
a new exotic dish for supper.

I know I will not cannot
read them, sort them, make them all
and yet I leave them,
in piles,
waiting.

The clothing hangs with hopes of
clinging to a smaller body
or perhaps the fashion will return
and I can dance again as once I swung
from branches in the sun.
The only true promise of time is that
I will grow more feeble
unable to remember
travelling from one room
to the next
what was my mission in the first place?
yet I still believe
I will complete the projects I have begun.

Every day
the light falls shorter in my window,
a mirage
that recedes
from my grasping
and only
makes me sadder
with its rosy hue.

Wild heart

Sally Churgel

We say to our dog sit and she sits
We say good girl and she wags her tail
We tame our horses by breaking them
In the same way we tame our hearts
Behave we say, good boy
You shouldn't say that, good girl
We say over and over, I am good
When a part of us believes I've been bad
Each belief is a whip to our flanks
Breaking our spirit
Cracking our hearts over and over

You ask forgiveness to others for the gossip,
Indifference and harm you caused them
You forget to ask forgiveness
For your critical self-slander,
The indifference and harm you cause yourself
By not listening to the still small voice within

Stop breaking your wild pony of a heart
Instead say to your good girl and good boy
I'm sorry

This year turn towards that brokenness
See it anew
Look beyond the broken latches and shards of glass
Created by your own sorrow
See openness

Climb through into the heart of your heart
To your untamed and uncivilized heart
Where the thrum of excitement and anticipation is loud
Enter your wild heart where thrives a teeming jungle of life

Monkeys howling with joy, swinging carefree above the
Grinning hyenas of shame, the ripping teeth of self-doubt
Here there are no civilized red lights
Here beyond brokenness only one light shines
The green light of love

Enter fully into the broken heart and you will find
Your whole, wild, untamed, uncivilized heart
Here there is only yes
Yes to love
Yes to life
Go deeply enough and you will remember
Your heart is the heart of the world
The world is the heart of God

The Year of Opposites

Diane Frank

Everyone gets into the truck. Also the goat.
      We have hay for the goat,
            a watermelon to slice for everyone else.
Everyone is dancing barefoot in Tiberius,
      watching the tourists baptize one another
            in the Jordan River.
Everyone is hoping a bomb won't go off
      when they visit Jerusalem –
            by the Wall or in a café
                in toss distance from
            a palm-size stone or a molotov cocktail.

Those days I was working with the gardener
      who spoke fluent Hebrew, Arabic and English
            at Kibbutz Yachad in the Northern Galilee.
It was better than working in the kitchen,
      where the cook, who only spoke Hebrew,
            would point to a huge pile of cucumbers,
                and say, *Green. Wash.*
Or a stack of red peppers –
      Red. Wash.
            Or a sink full of pots.
            Wash.

I spoke Hebrew with the Palestinian taxi driver
      who didn't know English.
He called the place I asked him to drive me
      Sof Olam – end of the world.
Two weeks later, everyone in Jerusalem
      swarmed the streets on Independence Day.
My friends told me that if a bomb
      was going to explode,
            it would be tonight and here.

The bomb went off in our neighborhood
       at 2:00 in the morning.
My dreams for the rest of the night –
       a Picasso mosaic of fractured gardens,
              light being sucked out of everything.
In Sfat, a Kaballist rabbi read my palm.
       He told me about the future I would avoid
              by leaving.

In a dream, I saw myself –
       a young woman with a scar,
              a field of tiger lilies, an ocean of sky.
A house with a balcony, maybe split timber,
       maybe redwood or white oak
              that grew long ago in a forgotten forest.
White deer ran through the garden –
       their bodies almost made of light.

Two weeks later, in Amsterdam,
       they detained me in the basement of the airport,
              found my suitcase on the tarmac,
walked me to the plane,
       took the magazine I was carrying out of my hand,
              made confetti of my future,
                     and sent me out of the war zone.

We didn't bend with the wind;
       we grew steel in our spines.
Every scar has an edge,
       a canyon, a crater of the moon.
In my house of dreams and split timber,
       I toss sunflower seeds in the garden,
              a shower of tiger lilies, oriental poppies.

I dig in my toes,
     and start to grow.
Life is a koan,
     and the most effective drum
         is the one that makes no sound.

I Know Love

Dianna L. Grayer

Every time I breathe.
Every time I lay in the sand,
And listen to the waves.
Feel the sun lightly on my face.
Hear the seagulls sing.
I know love.

When I journey through the woods
amongst the tall trees.
And then I pause to feel their embrace.
In return I embrace them.
I know love.

When I sit by the stream,
And listen to the diversity of sounds,
The music.
Nature's music.
I know love.

When I'm discontent,
feeling low, in need,
I go to a place that I can count on.
The mother who is steady.
Arms, always open,
Mother Earth.
She meets me where I'm at.
She loves me just the way I am.
All she asks is for me to love her.
And so I do, every time I breathe.

Let Me be Healed

Dianna L. Grayer

May the pain I suffer serve me.
Have it be for a good cause.
I yearn to understand its purpose - the outcome.
Let me know what I need to know.

May it be swift.
This pain, this constant ache.
This knowledge, this knowing.
May it be swift. May it be swift.
Creator, my Spirits, may it be swift.

I know life cannot be without hardship.
I know it can be difficult and full of struggle.
This I know.
But help me withstand the pressures and the pain,
find ways to remove the strife
living and dwelling where it need not be.

Let me see what I need to see.
Feel what I need to feel.
Address what I need to address.
Learn what I need to learn.
Help me to release toxins from my mind,
From my body, from my spirit,
And set my soul free.

Let me be healed in your light
And the light of the earth.
Thank you for this earth,
The earth that sustains me,
That fills me up with abundance.
Spirit, watch over me and help me on this journey.
Let me be healed.

II.

Margo Miller

This is my idea of heaven:
I step out of the shelter into the rain
I'm standing in a rain of blessings
My soul knows what it's doing
Holding on and letting go—they are the same

Within Me

Myrna Joy

Like the waters of the river,
running through the land so wide
to the sea's edge,
ever merging with the ocean's ebbing tide.

Like the motions of the high tide,
like the motions of the low,
so my love is this eternal,
growing warm with inner glow.

My love shall keep eternal,
through the high times and the low,
and like the waters in the river
shall run and grow,
shall run and grow,

until it becomes a river,
and only you can see
that the waters of this river
are running deeply within me.

Blankety Blank Page

Phil Temko

The poem that refuses to come in
From the cold to warm itself
Before the soul's still glowing hearthfire

No message this morning from the mind
To the impatient heart
Telling of its likely time of arrival.

Where's this morning's simile which
Like a nuthatch creeps headfirst
Down the tree trunk to the ground
Of my being?

Or the oddly missing metaphor
O patio squirrel scarfing up
Sunflower seeds, then vanishing
Up the tree, among the branches of my imagination!

Where the hell are you, poem?
I leave my window open –
wide, wide open.

Dancing Shoes and Kleenex

Sheridan Gold

I am not afraid. I am full of love and music.

This is my gift. Music has been there, all along, just waiting
for me to let it out. It's like that, waiting.
The notes, lingering,
The rhythms quietly pulsating, yearning to be heard.

Music.

It's the one thing that can unite everyone who is in its
presence without any kind of coercion or conversion.

Music is seduction. It seduces one into grounded-ness.
It gently urges one to listen, deeply listen to their inside.
It gently nudges the soul out of hiding.
It is there, waiting with dancing shoes or a box of Kleenex.
It has no expectations.

Tonight, I am the deliverer.
We are all deliverers.
There are no wrong notes.
There are no words or moves that are better or less than
    others.
Let them out.
Let them all out.

Tonight, we are the deliverers of this gift of music,
  to help those who are

listening,
laughing,
zoning out,
crying,
dancing,
healing.

We are here, delivering this gift that we are so privileged
    to hold.
It will no longer be ours exclusively.
Nor should it be.

Music has been there all along,
waiting for us to give it voice,
and give it away –
give it to those who need it,
who will be better for it,
and we shall all,
all of us,
heal our hearts
just a little bit more
than
yesterday.

The Ancestors

אבות ואמהות

Jacobs Family Seder 1939, Irwin Keller

My Dad

Nancy Rapp

Scent of sawdust,
Handmade wooden tables.
Compassionate carpenter.

Flight

Anna Belle Kaufman

A robin slammed
into my window last night.
with a sound like a shot.
The room shook
as she flew full throttle
into a mirage of clear blue freedom.
I ran to find her on her back
wildly thrashing, her tail
a flashing gray fan
against the red bricks,
her legs bent awry,
before she stilled.
My heart broke a little,
caught again
between love and helplessness.

I thought of my mother
watching me soar into first marriage.
At the wedding, her face betrayed
her fear it was a funeral.
Nonetheless, unasked, she'd cooked for days,
platters of her flaky piroshki,
her thin buckwheat blini
with sour cream and caviar.

At times our loved ones fly,
fueled by fervor
and innocence, towards a phantom.
Do we hold our hearts open?
Do we bend over our stoves for them?

Can we love ourselves, give thanks,
when we stand again on wobbly legs
shake our wings, head for
another piece of sky?

Do we pray for the robin
who collided too soon, too hard,
who lay cold and alone,
carried off by a predator in the night?

A Revisit

Rita Rowan

My Dad, a dark haired, brown eyed people person
   Knew what a knee crossed over a seated bent leg meant.

He recognized darting eyes in a presentation,
   Or fixed gazes,
And slightly nodding heads
Bobbing their approval.

He had a people filter, a good one.

He said too that he would return in the future
   To applaud my Mom
Her reincarnated self,
      A ballerina on the New York stage.

He had a people filter, a good one, loving my
   Mama.

Today, his great-grandson with my Mama's
      Spun gold hair, age seven,
Stands before me in a Mexican restaurant.
 Sparkling corn-flower blue eyes stare up at me.
   Not dark brown ones.

I get up to hold a door for a woman on crutches.
   Her black booted leg barely skims the floor.
      Impeding her steps,

         A heavy rectangular red purse dangles and
            opens like Pandora's box.

I pull out a chair for her, settle her down slowly.

My grandson watches and stares.
"Grammy, that was very nice of you.
    You put her in that chair so carefully
        Like a mama bird
            Touching her baby in a nest."

I see my father then, a people person,
    Applauding from the fifth row center,
        An old family story.

Bubbee

Susan L Miller

Bubbee

Peddling your milk
Pushing the wagon

A *glaszelah* milk
Pour me some too

Misers of your village,
Mintz Gebarnah

Preparing *piroshki*
Rolling challah dough for *Shabbas*

Tasting the *imberlach**
Polishing the candle sticks

A piece of chicken
A piece of meat
A clean dress
Shabbas is here

Imberlach   carrot ginger candy

My Mother

Yoná Flemming

She walked
between breaths,
a shadow
her face
hardened with
sorrow
and shame

her womanhood
denied,
she dried up and hung
in the wind
a whisper

But lately
my mother reminds me
of a desert flower
that blooms only once
and This Is Her Time

My mother has reached
up and watered
herself
giving me a gift
of growing

We have become
    sisters

Taking comfort

נַחֲמוּ נַחֲמוּ

Calla Lily, Leiah Bowden

Grief Storm

Cyndi Norwitz

Not yet a storm.
A swirl of dust, invisible at first
Catches the light and disappears.

Colors mute; it's just the sleep in my eyes.
Sound fails to carry; it's just these aging ears.

The dust grows thicker.
I start to curl within myself.
Has it come at last?

This year makes ten.
Ten trips around the sun without him.

Dust fills my room.
I reach out and see
My arms full of nothing.

My muscles ache with the effort
My eyes, my ears, my heart
Everything aches.

Ten years and here it is again.
The storm that never fails to find me.

A Few Stops Along the Way

Nancy Rapp

She watered the sterling-silver roses
With her tears of crystal,
Of pearl.
When it was all just too much
Of everything,
She looked over her shoulder to the western
edge
of the county that she
called home.
She remembered that the salmon still ran
In the pewter-colored river.
And in her heart, there was honey.

August Bar Mitzvah

Anna Belle Kaufman

He'd be thirty years this month,
the boy I lost so long ago.
His visage frozen at five,
smiling at me over his shoulder,
gripping the handlebars of his red trike
from behind a rectangle of glass.

Years have muted the pain
the way a brush dipped in water
melts the gash of colorstroke
and sweeps it across the paper
ever paler as it fans farther out.

For the children who do not stop growing
that first climb to the summit of the jungle gym,
the elation of the slide down,
becomes a graduation,
an engagement,
a fellowship,
a marriage,
a baby.

And each rite of passage, heard or witnessed,
shocks the calm waters of my old grief

like the paint-engorged brush
drops color into the clear rinse
which blooms with sudden
swirls of crimson or,
today, the cerulean blue
of the striped tallit he'd never wear.

Cold Solace

Anna Belle Kaufman

When my mother died,
one of her honey cakes remained in the freezer.
I couldn't bear to see it vanish,
so it waited, pardoned,
in its ice cave behind the metal trays
for two more years.

On my forty-first birthday
I chipped it out,
a rectangular resurrection,
hefted the dead weight in my palm.

Before it thawed,
I sawed, with serrated knife,
the thinnest of slices —
Jewish Eucharist.

The amber squares
with their translucent panes of walnuts
tasted — even toasted — of freezer,
of frost,
a raisined delicacy delivered up
from a deli in the underworld.

I yearned to recall life, not death —
the still body in her pink nightgown on the bed,
how I lay in the shallow cradle of the scattered sheets
after they took it away,
inhaling her scent one last time.
I close my eyes, savor a wafer of
sacred cake on my tongue and
try to taste my mother, to discern

the message she baked in these loaves
when she was too ill to eat them:
I love you.
It will end.
Leave something of sweetness
and substance
in the mouth of the world.

The Muted Man

*Diana Glassma*n

Who were you my four eyed glasses wearing
shiny headed old man

who all of his life
walked so fast
no one could keep up,
but in the end just shuffled.

The man who had such a
powerful
handshake
that other men
would cringe
and show stunned faces
when you shook
their hands,
but in the end
you just
sat there
plastered
into your favorite
red upholstered chair holding the pink rubber ball
that I bought you, squeezing it
trying
to get back
a little hand
strength
so that maybe
you could hold a pencil
again.

Yes you were the one who sat
with me
on those dirty
old steps
in the hallway
of our walk up
when I cried
because I wanted a dog so badly
and
she wouldn't let me have one,
you'll have a dog one day
I promise you said
to the little
begging girl,

later you would take
my small hands
into your large ones
and soap and soap
in that chipped white
rusty ringed sink
to get them clean,
so you taught me
how to wash
 my hands
and I loved
the feel
of your big hands enveloping
my small ones while I watched
the bubbles go down the drain.

And you told me those
endless stories
of the Summer
you left your parents' home

to hitchhike out West
for the adventure
for the getting
away

for the finding
of yourself,
you were a young man maybe 20 years old
and you spoke
those hitchhike stories over and over
and over
again
till the stroke
cut you down
and you became
a muted man.

I wish I could ask you and I wish
you could answer, who were you
when
the dark rage
the tumbling rage the growling rage
the rage
that overtook
and left
me weak
in the bladder,
and left
my brother pummeled
black and blue,
who were you then old man?

I wish you could tell me
I wish
you could

Grocery Store Kaddish

Irwin Keller

I mourn you in the grocery store
I say *Kaddish* in the asparagus
I see your eyes somewhere around the deli, by the kaiser
rolls
The single serving wine bottles and the too-soft sliced
cheese
I see your mostly empty fridge
Eating for one never became natural
Never drew your effort
This late time in life was for leaning back
For the easy meal on the snack tray
Work was done.
Marriage. Child rearing.
Peanuts, now unsalted, still the naughty treat.
Your footprints are here in the immensity
Of an over-chilled suburban supermarket
And here I say *Kaddish* in the produce,
Baruch Dayan Ha'emet in the frozen foods.

Time and Seasons
מוֹעֲדִים לְשִׂמְחָה

Blackbirds at Wilbur Hot Springs, Adam Shemper

Torah Study

Basha

    (upon learning that ark in Hebrew is also the word for box)

What is your offering?
When you step out of the box you are in
Moist pliant willing earth beneath you
Ready for planting ready for life
What smoke do you send
To the heavens
Thanking God for saving you
Once again.

Noah was stuck on that ark
which really was a box –a *'teyvah'*
waters raged around him, springs
filled up overflowed and he and
all he had gathered
floated
on the waters.

Then God remembered Noah
    (What was God busy doing that He forgot?)
and a wind blew over the earth
'Ruach' means wind breath and soul
and every breeze that blows through us
as we shiver here
above the deep waters.

Noah waited
until God said
"come out Noah come out"
And when he did the first thing he did was
make an offering, a barbecue for God.

How can the window of my mind open
to allow the Divine
to stream into my heart?

How can I step out
when God says "come out come out,
come out of your box
into the light
make your offering and
be happy
you are saved again from destruction
you are saved."

Who will remember to tell me
Floating in the deep
"The land can hold you,
The waters have subsided
And now it is up to you
To keep the covenant you made
And remember."

We were promised
"never again.
I will let you be.
I will let you multiply
and enjoy
the fruits of this place."
                        And yet it has happened
Again and again and again
Civilizations wiped out
Nothing left.

Jonah warned the people of Nineveh
and they repented of their selfish ways.
But we just laugh and feast

and send noxious smoke up to the heavens
relying on a promise made
to an old man in a box -
this covenant will not hold.
No rainbow can tie it up
like a birthday ribbon
around our little life on earth.

And how will we be remembered
and by whom?
How can we open the window
of the Ark we have fashioned
to protect us
from the angry flood
and the raging fire,
step out onto dry land
and be free.

What is your offering?
When you step out of the box you are in
Moist pliant willing earth beneath you
Ready for planting ready for life
What smoke do you send
To the heavens
Thanking God for saving you
Once again.
What is your offering?

Shofar Soundings

Barbara Lesch McCaffry

T'kiah, the sound reverberates to the inner core,
Calling us, in us, to listen deeply, delve inside —
stop   cease   savour —
as it scatters to silence.

I.
Malchuyot – The Divine Rules in Us

T'kiah, the sound that calls us to justice,
To caring for the peoples of this planet,
For the life forces that encircle us, both animate and
    inanimate—
the pebbles underfoot,
the rush of water,
the breathe of wind,
the embrace of sun that turns us beyond ourselves to listen,
T'kiah,
to act from our hearts,
to live in harmony
to act justly, not just for ourselves.

The sound echoes and enters us:
T'kiah ~ Shevarim T'ruah ~ T'kiah.

II.
Zichronot – Remembrance

The sound unheard, yet harkened:
a whisper of wind,
a murmur of water,
the prayers of our hearts.
The words leave our lips and float outward.
Listen, *T'kiah*.

They are heard beyond us,
reverberate in the world,
spark in us, in all of us,
the will to nurture actions that preserve, transform,
    transcend—
T'kiah ~ Shevarim ~ T'kiah.

III.
Shofarot – The Divine Redeems

The sound builds within and around us:
enfolding, embracing, enhancing our awareness,
connecting us to all creation,
healing our broken hearts,
inspiring us as we breathe in the notes,
holding each and holding us as community, as humans on
    this journey of discovery.
It implores us to embody, to include, to move beyond our
    selves.

As the shofar calls, lifting us, filling us,
may we echo its intent in our lives and in this world.
T'kiah ~ Teruah ~ T'kiah Gedolah

Shabbos-Fall in British Columbia

Irwin Keller

It's nearly Shabbos in British Columbia.

People sit in traffic on their way to dates and movies. They fiddle with the car radio and check the time on their cell phones.

Some have just gotten home, closing the door on the hard week. They drop bags and jackets and receive the embrace of well-worn armchairs.

Some Jews set tables and stir pots of soup like their grandmothers before them, except that jazz is playing and the soup has kale and some of the stirrers are men.
In this pink twilight people hurry, turn on TVs, pour wine, open books. Dogs, elated, emerge into their evening walks, sniffing grass and trees and each other, tails curled in a question mark.

Even in the tall city sheathed in asphalt the trees outnumber the people. The flowers outnumber the cars. The grass stretches from one end of the province to the other, from Pacific to Rockies – each blade of it has a melody. If that melody had words, it might sound like "reach" or "dig" or simply "I am." "I am," sings the grass.

A pair of angels – great, translucent and multicolored like rainbows on soap bubbles – survey the scene. They eye the whole province: seagulls shrieking over fishing boats; pencils working crossword puzzles and couples dozing on sofas; traffic roaring; Jews singing *Lecha Dodi*, rivers clapping over rocks; grass reaching; owls waking; all of life breathing.

The angels survey all of this, Shabbat falling in British Columbia. One angel dissolves into a prayer, which if it were in words, would go: "So may it be again next week."

At which the other angel bursts into a scent of lilac, which if it were in words, would go: "*Ken yehi ratzon,* may it be so."

And the grass responds, "I am."

Avodah (Service)

Cyndi Norwitz

The first of the final three blessings of the Amidah

I built my house from goat hair on poles.
Opened a flap and offered you bread
With milk to drink down your promises
And plant them for later.

I built a house from mud, sweat, and straw.
For one frightening night
You sheltered with me
Then led me to a place without bricks.

I built you a house from acacia and gold.
Be-jeweled and be-wildered
You stayed
And wandered the desert with me.

I built you a house of stone
To stand for a thousand years.
I catch glimpses of you
In the rubble.

Now I build you houses of pine and oak
Beaten metal and gypsum
Spires to catch the sun
Shingles to roll the rain.

In this house I built, may the work of my breath
Fill you with longing
To plant your feet in the dust of a thousand prayers
And dwell.

The Scent of Shechinah

Irwin Keller

In the journey in the desert,
What will you be?
Goatherd? Guide? Gopher?
Priest? Prophet? Perfumer?

There in the wilderness,
Amid scrub and thorns,
To make a *mishkan*,
A holy pop-up
Sanctuary
Where tablets are kept
And where *Shechinah* dwells,
Will you share your arts?

Your clever fingers shuttling the
Fine yarns and dyes. Making curtains and covers.
Beams and basins. And gold cherubim,
Face to face, framing the Divine face between.

Will you make it not just a feast for the eyes
But one for the nose as well?
A place for ascent through scent?

Torah gives the recipe:
Take 500 shekels of myrrh, says God,
Half that much of cinnamon, a spice so old
That even in Torah it is already called *kinneman*.
Another 250 of *k'neh* – calamus root?
And 500 of *kiddah* – that's cassia, another bark with
    some bite.

Grind to a pulp, Torah hints, then blend
With olive oil to make a rich balm
That is not burned but rubbed
On altar and ark and lampstand and utensils
Greasing the fittings with good-smelling goop.
These are not like the fragrances of today.
Today, chemicals cooked in corporate labs
Are carrier waves for smells that might once
have had something to do with nature. Possibly.
Or maybe not even.

But in this old time. In the desert.
Scents were devised with sensibility.
Mortar and pestle. Delights olfactory
Made of industry but no factory.
A time when the word "natural"
Was not needed before "fragrance"
Because what else would it be?
Things smelled of what they were.
The perfume smelled *of* cinnamon,
It did not smell *like* cinnamon,

Not like now, not like the reek
Of detergents and soaps and candles
And air fresheners – toxic mimics
Of nature, slowly degrading
in bathroom dispensers
or plugged into walls,
Or worst of all, in a taxi, from which there is no escape
While the meter racks up in dollars and cents
The cost of breathing this offense.

But not in the desert *Mishkan* of old:
One part cinnamon, two parts myrrh,
Cassia, calamus, oil.
Stir.

We never know how we'll serve until we get there.
But what if it were *you* whose job
Was to make the perfume?
What if this were your service,
The product of your wise heart,
Your skilled fingers,
Your much maligned Jewish nose.
You, the *rokeach*, the aromatist!
You whose work is to waft
What Yahweh wants to whiff?
At the end of your long day, crushing, stirring,
Anointing all that is holy,
Pans, poles and priests,
Would you come home empty-handed
As God commanded?
Or would you risk retribution
And sneak some for yourself –
A trace behind the ear?
A drop in the soft of your wrist?
As enticement for a lover.
As invitation to a dream.
As memory of Shechinah.
And a reminder that you too are God?

A Day of Rest

Laura Blatt

Begin at sunset
with challah and candles
dinner for two or more
praise on printed pages
a book of poems

Turn off
phones
computers
all electronics.
Turn up inner voice.

At sunrise enjoy
luscious strawberries
so sweet
so fragrant
in oatmeal with cream.

With sunshine and curiosity
observe the Goddess of
creeks and ferns
connect with heart
arrive at yet another sunset.

Avot v'Imahot — Ancestors Interpretative Variation

Cyndi Norwitz

Baruch Atah Adonai, Eloheinu v'Elohai avoteinu v'imoteinu
(Please take one step forward)

God of our founders, our legends, our sacred myths
God of our matriarchs, our patriarchs,
    our voices of Torah and prophecy
(Please take one step forward)

God through the Diaspora, of our homelands
    throughout the world
God of our Rabbis, our healers, our teachers, our leaders
God of those too far back for memory
(Please take one step forward)

God of our ancestors within our lifetimes
    and of blessed memory
God of those who held and shaped us
God of those near enough to imagine
(Please take one step backward)

Remember the love of our mothers and fathers!
(Please take one step backward)

Remember the sacrifices of our ancestors through history!
(Please take one step backward)

*Melech ozeir umoshia umagen. Baruch atah, Adonai, magein
Avraham v'ezrat Sarah.*
Sovereign, Deliverer, Helper and Shield, Blessed are You,
Adonai, Sarah's Helper, Abraham's Shield.

Cakes

Shoshana Fershtman

Once
We baked cakes for the queen of heaven
And called You by name—Astarte, Asherah,
Goddess
Anat, our protector

Jeremiah told us the famine came
Because we honored you.
And we answered: "We shall not listen to you.
For when we poured libations
and burned incense to the Queen of Heaven,
and baked her cakes,
we had plenty of food and saw no evil."

But Jeremiah's ways prevailed,
And we,
We have gone hungry ever since

In the temple, your likeness stood for over 200 years
Though many tore you down,
We restored you,
Again, and again
An ancient tug of war that we had hoped,
Mistakenly, was finally coming to an end

You joined us in our exile
As Shekhinah
We no longer called you Asherah, happy,
Because how could we be,
With your House in ruin?

Your sacred vulva,
Once celebrated in menarche rites and child birthing
Reflected in the cleft of trees
The mouths of caves

Your likeness,
Clutched by Zilpah as she gave birth to Asher,
Secreted by Rachel as she left her father's house,
The downward facing triangle,
Was buried deep,
Trampled over with centuries of forced forgetting
It was only after the Shoah
When so many lost our faith in the G-d on high
Did you return to us,
Thousands of your likenesses
Springing up in ancient digs
Throughout the motherland

You whispered to us,
"Here I have been all along,
Buried deep in the soil,
Buried deep in *your* earth."

"I have always been here," You remind us,
"Hidden."

Astarte / Queen of Heaven
Nistar / Hidden
Esther / Queen

I smile when I see you in your pink pussy hat,
The downward facing triangle
Reclaimed, celebrated!
Delighting as the two ears reach out to heaven,
Your chin forming the third angle
Pointing to the belly of the mother.

And I think, "Now *those* are hats!"

But as I look down
At my plate of hamantaschen,
Gleaming with
Juicy raspberry jam,
Succulent apricots,
And poppyseeds ground
In the mortar and pestles of the grandmothers,
I think,

These are NOT hats!

These are cakes,
Cakes luscious enough to sate the hunger of millennia
Cakes for the Queen of Heaven.

Annulment of Vows

Shoshana Fershtman

After a lifetime of sucking at the toxic teat of
    not-good-enough
After a year's dark night of disillusion
I formally renounce my collusion
With the false idols of unattainable perfection
And its faithful consort, self-loathing

I annul my vows
G!d is perfect
And I, human, gather my true self
From the scattered shards of my broken heart

In a year where some of us have had to surrender
everything
Torn from us
By life and circumstance
Stripped bare,
We reach for what is real and enduring

Shekhinah,
Gather my brokenness
Beneath the shelter of your wings
Anoint me with the balm of Your loving presence

Our Sukkot celebrations marred by flames
We had a deeper empathy
For children ripped from parents
Huddled in foil blankets
Offering no comfort.

And the other flames too, lit by human hands
Tiki torches of hatred
Summoning visions of Kristallnacht

In Gaza, our brothers and sisters,
Esau, Ishmael, felled by our own hands,
As we pray seemingly in vain for the long-sought reunion
S'lach lanu, mechal lanu, kaper lanu

Strengthen us for a year when everything
hangs in the balance
Our mother plundered by small minds and greedy hands
Heedless of the devastation they unleash

Turn me from those who would seduce me
with false comforts
And bind me to the real
Create for me a pure heart,
and renew a steadfast spirit within me.

This new year is a mikveh
My soul washed clean

Oh Holy Blessed One,
Bathe me in the river of Your healing light
That flows from forever
Into the eternal now

For A B' Mitzvah*

Shoshana Fershtman

At this time of Tu Bishvat,
We plant trees for the future
To blossom generations after we are gone.

I wonder, what blessings can we offer you,
to strengthen you for the tasks ahead
to prepare you for the world you will steward?

We give you our hearts, broken open through love
transformed through suffering
that we hope has matured into compassion

We offer you your ancestors' wisdom
Guided by "justice justice" *tzedek, tzedek*, shall you pursue
The words that hang above RBG's desk
and our Exodus story that teaches that deliverance comes
in the most dire of times

And the deep knowing of your other ancestors,
wisdom bearers from Stonehenge to Stonewall,
Langston Hughes, Gandhi and Rosa Parks,
Know that they too surround you
To call on for their insight.

Most of all we give you our faith, and our hope in you.
You are the blossoming of prayers planted by your
ancestors decades and centuries ago.
You are the blossoming of prayers planted by your
ancestors centuries and eons ago.

For it was only the generation born in the desert
after leaving Egypt
That entered the promised land
Because their hearts and minds were free.
And know that we are with you, listening with bated
breath
And watching with hearts aflutter
Cheering as you step into your adulthood
because YOU are the future of earth.

Our hearts race when we hear the students of Parkland
Calling BS on those who, driven by greed,
stand in the way of a more just and peaceful future.
Inspiring students across the country to march, to change
minds and change laws.

And even though we are trembling at the world you are
entering,
Know that in that trembling is not only fear
but also awe and excitement at what might be possible
because of the vision you carry, a vision that far exceeds
our own.

Written for Addison Reid Brown for his B Mitzvah on January 19, 2019

Song of Miriam

Leiah Bowden

I took him to the river, my baby brother.

The birds were singing and the river, as always, drew me in, my friend, my river.

He didn't cry, my baby brother, and I rocked him in his water-cradle.

One hand on the basket rim and the other drumming the rhythm of my heart on the sunwarmed riverskin, I gave the river my command.

"I am here, I of your own nature, water to water. Water to water, I give you my brother, my sweet boy, and I charge you with carrying him on your breast as if he were your own wave. I, water to water, your own, I charge you with this."

He didn't cry, my baby brother, and my river-servant rocked him in his water-cradle.

The birds were singing, and I followed, water in water, watching the wave of my future float downstream where birdsong turned into women's laughter.

I watched the water and the waterbasket and the waterboy and the sunlight blazing upon the wave and the watching One breathed upon the water and I drew in my breath as she drew forth my baby brother and held him, heart to heart and then of course she could not let him go and for the rest of her life she was his, as he was ours.

My water-borne brother could command the water as ever did I, for the command I gave water, water speaking to water, had no expiration date.

But this time, my drum was the heartbeat of a multitude.

And so we crossed, so many years later, water giving way to water.

Not such a surprise.

A Yom Kippur Melody

Rita Rowan

I sing with my mother's voice, a voice that passed
   long ago.
I sing this Yom Kippur, this day of atonement.

I sing my family's song,
   Some buried in the earth's
     Snow blanketed winter ground
      Barely shifting their energy into
     Surrounding California Oaks
Whose gnarled branches grasp for winter souls.

Some are here
Walking the Sonoma creekside leaf laden paths,
  Still inhaling the ashes of burned homes,
   Great Grandma Rebecca's Holocaust brass candlesticks
   Chagall lithographs bought at auction
    By my son Leigh
whose baby pictures stored in my garage
      During the October blaze
      Melted too.

I hear my mother's voice still resonating among the rubble
   Her perfect pitch
Her voice soaring clear
  Steady and calm

I hear alto tones echoing back
 As I sing the Aleynu
 At times, only some times,
  Quivering

Lest I be off key.

Ten Decades Celebration of Our Cotati Shul Home Building on Pomo Miwok Ground

Robin Birdfeather

dancing Torah folks
deepen new world Jewish soul
Cotati vibrates

two old worlds meet
our tent of ancient timbers
 multiply blessings

songs stories dancing
 new mishpochah celebrates
widening wisdom

communal hearts thrum
 brave minds discover more roots
 in the meeting tent

Relationships

קֶשֶׁר

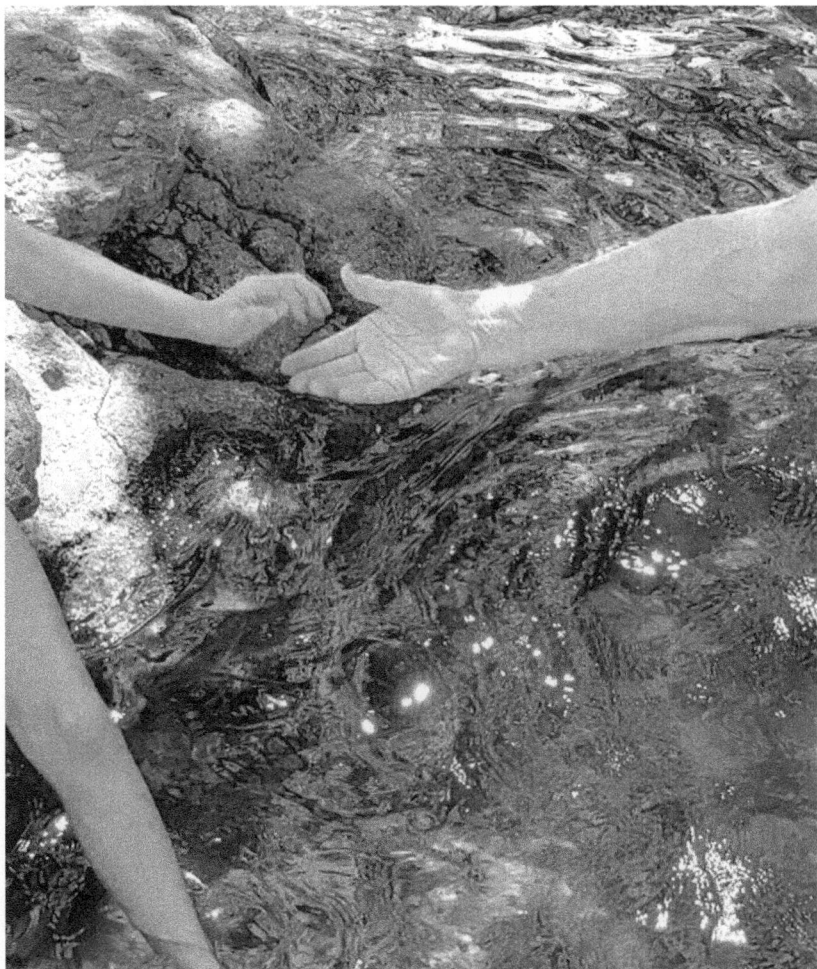

Trust in the Stream, Seth Bowden

Sitting with Lee

Leiah Bowden

Good will lined with longing for what was
and
or
what could still be if only
settles on us, companionably couched
on a moist summer evening,
unspoken as we talk
about the laundry, hairy moles on old women,
someone's braided ear hair
and report each to the other on our day

Your eyes look large behind your reading glasses
and I see your body shake
when your tremoring hand rests behind your head.
but we've covered that already

We marvel at the sparrow
nesting on my front porch wind-chime
nested as we are,
arms and legs
casually touching
on the couch on which
I rarely sit
alone.

Even This Late (Kintsugi)

Margo Miller

A piece of cracked china can be mended
Not like new, never like new, but strong and usable
Even that which is inflammable can be burned
Even that which is immutable
Even that which is indelible
Even that for which it is too late.
Even too late, perhaps the damage can be repaired:
Even this late, it happens.

Fare Well

Basha

leaving on a trip
is a little like dying:
the last meal cooked,
the last sunset,
the leather chair
still bearing your form
like a silhouette.

soon you will be gone
but who knows quite how long
the revolving door
swings round and
the dishes are put
on their shelves.

the golden haze of afternoon
leaves a crimson kiss.
sky slowly darkens.
fragile
as the first star
of evening,
a promise of return.

Strong Ties

Dafna Jo Simon

To say that we're friends isn't saying enough.
We're a feeling better left unsaid.
My life in a vision is a woven stuff
and each time I know you
see in a pattern
emerging, essential, one thread
Becoming...

Say that we're music, a song to be sung.
I'm a melody all my own,
the harmony of us blending into one
notion of balance
hear as we sing us
emerging, essential, unknown
Becoming...

Strong ties whenever you're here.
More and more distance
is bringing you near.
The times we're together
quelling my fear
of bonds being broken
and words left unspoken ---
Hey, look, we're still open!
Connection clear.

Say we're a rainbow, touching land, reaching stars.
Oh, beloved child of sunshine and rain
the colors created are uniquely ours
as perception we touch us
intangible something
emerging, essential refrain,
Becoming...

Strong ties whenever you're here.
More and more distance
is bringing you near.
The times we're together
quelling my fear
of bonds being broken
and words left unspoken ---
Hey, look, we're still open!
Connection clear.

Ruthless Mah Jongg

Rita S. Losch

Humid Jersey summer nights:
my father in boxer shorts comfortable
in the air conditioned master bedroom
with his snacks, his wide world of sports,
remotely controlling boxing or bowling,
my kid brother hiding in his blue bedroom,

I sat invisibly around the bend at the top
of the carpeted stairs, smelling the coffee,
hearing the clicking and constant chatting
of my mother's weekly mah jongg game below,
and entirely baffled by the game's lingo.

All over, Jewish children at the tops of stairs
sat fascinated, mesmerized and bewildered
while their mothers with frosted hair,
cherry red fingernails and hot pink Capri pants
sat at card tables with chartreuse quilted pads,
ate snacks, talked bar mitzvahs and sweet sixteens,
playing swiftly and smoothly an ancient Chinese
men's game, the Game of the Sparrows.

Up north, it was Rose, Edna, Adele, and Lil.
Here in Florida, it is Lil and the three Ruths.
They sit north, east, south and west,
each with her change purse (faux leather,
gold lamé, snazzy silk, an old Sucrets tin),
shuffling the clinking ivory tiles: four Winds,
three Dragons (the white Dragon they call Soap),
Dots, Bamboos or Bams, Craks, puzzling
Flowers used as Jokers or Deuces Wild.

82

They build walls of face-down yellowed tiles
up against the maroon and jade racks,
"curtsey" to push their walls out for courtesy
pick and discard tiles, calling what they throw,
exchange the first confusing Charleston,
get a weird Pung if they have a Bouquet Hand,
Kong Out, or make a Quint or Sextette
or throw a Flower to Dog a Hand.

They sit for Mah Jongg until
a Ruth declares Mah Jongg in error or
another Ruth finally makes Mah Jongg
or they call a Wall Game.
Looking ahead or picking ahead
is absolutely not allowed.

Between games they ask,
"If you had called the Green,
would it have sent you?"
They say, "Oy Gottenyu."
They ask, "Which Ruth?"
They say, "In the Cold Wall,
you can throw anything, and
you can't call it:
if you want to go Mah Jongg,
you need to pick it yourself."
Between games they say,
"I had to pass my Flower."

I sat upstairs utterly befuddled.

To my mother, Lillian Strauss Losch.

I.

Margo Miller

I have spent all the years of my life
gluing fragments into something
using fierceness as my glue

Oh my family!
If the living waters dissolve it, how can we stay connected?

Maybe on that day
it will break my heart
and make me whole.

Baruch ata adonai she'asani bat chorin.

Praise

פְּסוּקֵי דְּזִמְרָה

Sacha in Big Sur, Adam Shemper

Holy Coats

Sally Churgel

God spun loamy soil full of earth
worm casings and dinosaur cells
with intergalactic dust and a photon or two to weave
a rainbow fabric that breathes air and repels water
Then fashioned coats with a holy perfection
One for each and every soul that would
ever, and has ever, been created

We call it our body

Some tend to leave their coat on the rack
while their soul tries to mediate the continual
bickering between their internal aspects
Most hang out on the rack,
their coat commutes to the office,
drinks double lattes, and avoids eye contact with strangers
A few wear the coat inside out or buttons off by one hole
Some keep their hands in their pockets all day,
the collar pulled up over their ears

We *are* allowed to wear this coat
like a cat stretched belly up in the morning sun
Or a hawk - diving down on a field mouse -
full of focus, deliberation and the sheer bliss of Being

We *can* throw the coat in the corner
wake up in the morning with a hangover
the book never written

We all slip out of our coats in our sleep
To dream
We are God dreaming
God is us in our coats

We forget that this is the truth

Someday God will take our coat back
It will be hung in a great marble palace
where we will want for nothing

Do not risk that you may want for one thing

Wear the coat now just in case one day you may long to
take that coat off its celestial hanger and wrap your soul
for just one more lingering, focused, deliberate and blissful
Moment of Being

God brings you into a new land

Sally Churgel

God brings you into a new land
Look, it's just over this hill
Not the one with ten miles of gridlock before your exit
Not even the hill covered with auburn grape vines

The hill between you and this new land
Is of your own creation
It's the hill made of spent dreams and regrets
Comparisons and despair

This hill is not as steep as it seems
It is covered with the sweet lilac scent of longing
You cannot walk this hill alone
The soft, yielding hand of the Shechina is always present

You shall not lack for anything in this land
This is a land of olive oil and honey
Where bread of every description abounds

Here, truth is like a fig, chewy and sweet
It's no longer like a pomegranate
With only small bursts of fleeting flavor
Here, your heart is as resilient as iron but as yielding
As a field of barley in a summer breeze

Your body and soul are entwined like
A dazzling vine of bronze stems and copper leaves
Even in this land you must be still in order to hear the
Sound of water flowing from deep springs

God brings you into a new land
But you still must walk
The wind will still blow in your face
Your heart can close again

If in the morning you wake and the hill is here again
Just put on your walking shoes
And climb again
And again, if need be

Remember you cannot climb this hill alone

Dreams of the Ecliptic

Diane Frank

To change a girl into a kite,
    tell her that love is the moon.

To teach a tree to sing,
    put a harp under its branches.

To change a bowl of dust into a planet,
    paint watercolor rings around the ecliptic.

To change the sky into a dream,
    put a song into a hammock.

To melt an ice cube,
    light a fire under the map of the constellations.

To write a symphony in a major key,
    plant a rainbow under an apple tree.

To create a universe,
    ride on a meteor shower
        as the archer shoots a path of light
            across the sky.

When the sun rises for the first time,
    fill the sky with your singing.

love is

Robin Birdfeather

love is
inspired by my shul sisters
and for my mother who was, and is

love
has to go somewhere
must reside so that it may do its work
is a moving force
must find many homes

unstoppable as gravity is
and without the weight
d'lighted to be the way light travels
mysteriously constant

penetrates the darkest spaces
with caresses of need
bonding like stars do
pebble by pebble
with the science of connection

resides everywhere sometimes an orphan -
parents unknown
may wander ceaselessly searching

nameless to a fault
lives within tears of joy
between the drops
invisible indivisible
beyond even the special power of neutrinos
that know no boundaries

leaps between knowings and beings
unleashes the special forces of existence
transcends the meager attempts of poets trying
to capture its essence

its own universe
beyond the solidness of rocks
    flying airless
  burning without heat
    flowing between droplets
    of waves

  beyond food
  chartless

food of souls, of all beings

timeless
no beginning
no end

Night Fishing

Terry Rowan

Like a curled elephant's trunk, the line is cast
overhead and out, the little weight a satellite
fired into the night sky and watery abyss

so far out the bait is tethered only by a faith,
a seeking beyond hope, a probe fueled by the
slightest possibility that some huge force,

dark, immense, mysterious, filled with meaning,
also seeks at the same moment its destiny in the
night. Oh, to shout in that sublime moment

"We are truly caught, each by the other." Yet,
atop the boat's hard deck, where the stars blink
with their vast indifference, where ancient waiting

is our true work, the pulling back the empty hook
is no less a message for its lesser weight: "Cast again,
Fool. And wait."

Drum Song

Yoná Flemming

river moves through
high graceful hills
river glides to sea
river moves

drums speaking with
hand-tongues
like the river-water-language
moving

sea-voice lifting from
steep foggy slope
shields of water
rising to explode

river water rushes into
pounding sound

drumming

Making Our Way Back

Sheridan Gold

For many of us, we were kids raised in a religion we didn't
understand,
or didn't agree with.
Yet we are here.

For many of us, Judaism was unfair - it didn't speak to us,
it didn't see us.
Yet we are here.

For girls and women, we saw our fathers and our brothers
and sons be given gifts of Tallit, Bar Mitzvah, Yarmulke,
and the reclining at Passover.
Yet, we are here.

For others, we saw the embracing of our straight brothers
and sisters in marriage,
but our love was invisible.
Yet, we are here.

We are here, brought together by the love of a religion that
we may not have embraced in our younger years, brought
together by the love of music, and brought together by the
love of each other.

We are walking testaments of standing the test of time.
We made our way.
We had children.
We had careers.
We had arguments.
We read, and laughed, and went on vacations, and partied.
We stayed far, far away.

And yet, we made our way back.
We made our way back to a community that embraces all
of our differences and says,
WELCOME

We made our way back to a community that says,
come - sit, relax, sing, pray, eat, laugh, love.

We made our way back.
We are in our 80s, 70s, 60s, 50s, and 40s, some of us are in
our teens. It doesn't matter. What matters is that we are
here. Here now.

> We made our way back.
> And we rejoice.

Written for and dedicated to Congregation Ner Shalom.

For Our Children

Alexandra Ellen Appel

see the way the cool air stays memory and shadow, light
blackened pine needles keeps the night

long past the dawn and the noon of day, long past
the song of June rises from the meadow

hear the press of brambles
and the rustle of timothy grass

the hot crush of sun falls in the deep wood
see how the pines crowd imagination with an intimation of
winter

where once an old ice house stood
and the spring fed pool endures ice late in summer

and the scent of the musky earth rises from this bog
and here is a clear pool of still water

hear the source, the old lay lines
beneath the accumulation of forest

here is the way of the world,
lawful in purpose.

On a day in summer hear a whisper
cup your hands, let
the holy water numb your fingers, let

the sweetness of mountain and memory
revive nearly forgotten joy

let the clear water escape
let the rivulets flow between your fingers

let the capture of sun filter the shadow. Let
the moment of life ripple across the water
and here is stillness

see the tremble beneath the surface, see the silence
see the innocence written on the rock.

Openings
שְׁעָרִים

Motel Inverness Window on Tomales Bay,
Adam Shemper

Mitzvah Maybe

Rita Rowan

A dark skinned young man drives his aging metallic car in
the beating rain
  Pulling up alongside my newer silver SUV
    On Fulton Road, Santa Rosa CA

No whistles nor beeps to warn him that his door is ajar,
 Dangling from his partially closed car door,
  the corner of his rain jacket,
   Captured by the wind.

I blow my horn. Once. Twice.
Roll down my window
Point my older white finger towards his vehicle
Point some more.

His window closed.
Mine down,
I shout

"Your door is open."
"Your door is open."

He looks at me.
Glaring.
Sneering.
Gives me the finger, a rocket projectile
Splayed against his closed window.
He curves his other fingers inward
Pressing his middle finger

ever higher
touching the cold glass.

A mile later
 Turning onto Route 12
  His old car
   Once again pulls alongside mine.

He reaches his lips and smiles
blows me a kiss.
Then motions to his unencumbered door.

grins and drives forward to greet the day
Leaving my windshield
splattered with rain
    as he passes.

Astronaut

Terry Rowan

O, this time
birth is an active verb,

the astronaut casting
out, feet first,

From the hatch
still tethered at all points

by the cord tied to the
mothership. Small jets

push him this way
to make an elementary repair.

Inside his pressure suit,
he looks at the blue turning

Earth, out there, remembers
as a baby the carnival, the

slow whirling light of the
Ferris wheel in the night.

My Inheritance

Linda Pantoskey

This is my inheritance:
All that breathes and flourishes
that improbably thrives
All that grasps this earth with bones and stalks
that will weary and bend
All that muses the senses
with scents sights sounds
humbling and whelming
Mine

Graced astoundingly
with this infinite inheritance
to waste a moment is to miss
Something Anything
Stay awake! Breathe deeply!
Plumb resolutely with
the finite number of breaths
inherited borrowed
bestowed
Mine

As creaks and gaps slack the hurry
tilt toward every hue, every aroma
savor adore
Welcome brilliance and ripeness
to soothe the creaks
to bless the gaps
sweetly softly
Mine

Tenderness unfurls as the weave loosens
as purpose wanes
Lust for what is expansive, vital
Vow to follow the color and waft
that suits this day, only

No color too saturated nor muted
no scent too strong, no chord too deep
never too much
of this feast
Mine

Margalit

Diane Frank

for Margalit Oved, Yemenite dancer and choreographer

"... The *duende* surges up from the soles of the feet... It is not a
matter of ability but of real, live form; of blood; of ancient
culture."
 Federico Garcia Lorca
 Theory and Function of the Duende

The younger dancer didn't have what she did—
the swaying of eucalyptus leaves in her fingers,
the taste of old world salt on her breath.
Margalit was like the flamenco dancer
with fire in her throat,
hibiscus on her lips,
belly swaying in the rhythm of the sea.

Yes, I know...
The violist who stopped performing
before the arc of his vibrato
passed its prime. The french horn player
who eased himself out of the opera
while his lips still had the ability to kiss his wife.
The ballerina who set up a dance academy
after her swan song.

Margalit said her protege
could execute subtle moves that her aging body
did not have the agility to perform,
but this is what I saw—
a young tree with hollow branches,
the flaming red and burnt umber
of the change of season

absent from her palette of painting oils.
Her movements lithe but lacking *duende*,
too much sunshine in her hands.

I wanted to feel
the spice of black olives in a Yemenite market,
the cucumbers and tomatoes,
the drum made from the recycled tin
that was filled with olive oil.
I wanted to feel the rhythm
of long boats pulling fish from the Mediterranean sea,
the nets of the fishermen.
I wanted to watch her veined and beautiful hands
gathering rosebuds from her mother's garden,
brass bells dreaming on her ankles
with the memory of the land where she was born,
and the way her mother carried her across the desert
to the Promised Land.

The Soul's Cry for Freedom

Dianna L. Grayer

The human suffering trance—

When the self ignores the self.
Destroys the self.
Denies the self,
Denies the truth
Or doesn't look for it.
Avoids reality,
Or is just plain afraid of it.

The soul, suffocated, cries for freedom.
The soul is Tired of the prison walls.
The soul is Tired of being hostage.
Not for a day or night,
But a lifetime.

Who told you to stay still?
Never to move, Never to listen,
Never to risk, Never to need,
Never to deserve, Never to demand?

Who told you you're not worthy when you are!
Who told you not to fight back when you can!
Who told you suffering was your fate when you can
change!
Who told you misery is your happiness when it's farthest
from the truth.

Suffering is not human nature.

Hear the cries.
Keep listening even though it's hard.
Even though it hurts.
Even though it's terrifying.

Let them flow, the tears.
For all the distracted years.

Follow the wisdom from your soul.
Be the person you were meant to be,
Not the person you settled on being.
Eviction of the old.
Spaciousness for the new.
Listen to Your soul's cry for freedom.
Freedom. Freedom.

Begin Now

Diana Glassman

Begin now
with the here and now
staying in it
planting your feet
down
in the earth
feel your skin warm
your bone strong
and hear only what's said,
not what you imagine
is said
and ask, if you are not sure
asking is freedom
it brings it all into focus
brings you the truth
not the garnishes
nor the embellishments
or the imaginings,
so look
look simply
into someone's eyes
and ask
ask for the here and now
to embrace you
to empower you
to grace you
so that
even when the past intrudes
or makes its undying presence
known,
you can love it
for its past essence
its past truth

and not carry it with you
layering on top
of your here and now.
The deep thick lumbering layers are there
and yes they deepen you
and you call upon them
when you need to
or want to,
but the path is not
to obscure the present
with their presence,
the path is there
to walk it now
begin now
step by step
footprint by footprint
only being
in this particular footprint
in this particular time

Adirondack High Peaks: Shekhinah's Lament

Leiah Bowden

I whispered I love you to the trees,
and they opened their leaves to the sun
and made chlorophyll for nourishment
and sent my love rustling through the air.

I lapped I love you to the streams
and their joy flowed
rushing in a thousand fluid notes
over mountain streams sunlapped dappled
through wooded glades.
Crawfish danced and minnows fanned.

I sang I love you to the babies
and they saw the world offering its presence,
eyes wide, fingers waving,
smiles that were not gas.

I wished I love you to the multitudes,
and they all shifted weight,
turned their eyes with lonely hope to each other
and yearned, "If only..."

I said I love you to my children as they worked
and their tears choked their interim reports.
I repeated I love you in their dreams
and they woke up hungry
for conversation.

I love you turns the people to the mountains,
it turns them to the shore,
it hollows out their fearful hearts.
What is the language in which I love you
turns them toward each other?

I cried I love you in all my pain
into the broad heart of the ocean
and it shattered my cry
on coral reefs, on resistant boulders,
splintered my cry into a billion shining droplets
and carried my love back to its faceless source.

Poets and Dreamers

Alexandra Ellen Appel lives in Petaluma. Recent work appears in Cirque: A Literary Journal of the Pacific Northwest and Cross Currents North: Alaskans on the Environment. For her University of Vermont Doctorate, she authored "A Philosophy of Education from an Ecopsychologic Perspective: An Argument for Teacher As An Eco-moral agent."

Robin Birdfeather: Poetry, soulwork. First remembered: nursery rhymes, classics in one-room country schoolhouses. Creating poems carries me in soul wrenching times my soul answers. Discovering haiku during cancer treatment - intense demanding playground sharpening my feelings around life and death. My poetry Muse, always there whenever I seek her.

Laura Blatt's writing has appeared in *Lilith, California Quarterly,* and *Pendora* magazines and several anthologies. She has worked as a website writer, a laboratory technician, and a publishing company manager. A member of the California Bar, Ms. Blatt also has a master's degree in biology.

Abby Lynn Bogomolny is the editor of the anthology *New to North America: Writing by US Immigrants Their Children and Grandchildren* and the author of the poetry collection *People Who Do Not Exist*. She teaches Literature and Creative Writing at Santa Rosa Junior College.

Leiah Bowden has been a lifelong peripatetic poet. A retired communications strategist and actor, she is also an essayist, artist specializing in soul energy portraits, animal communicator, spiritual counselor, supporter of her beloved Ner Shalom, mother and Nana. She shares her life on www.lightspeak.com.

Sally Churgel is Ner Shalom's Yom Kippur yizkor leader, poet laureate from 2009-2019, and past president. Sally is a healer/intuitive, writer, and transformation guide. Her business, *Call to Joy*, was founded for those who yearn to live with joy as your base note rather than a rare and random experience.

Yoná Flemming has written poetry since she was a teen (now 78), and has pursued many other art forms. She studied, taught and performed Afro-Cuban drumming/music for 35 years. She treasures her Jewish roots. She has a large and wonderful family.

Shoshana Fershtman, JD, PhD, is a Jungian analyst and psychologist in private practice in northern California. She serves on the spiritual leadership committee at Congregation Ner Shalom. Her book, *The Mystical Exodus in Jungian Perspective: Transforming Trauma and the Wellsprings of Renewal*, was published by Routledge in 2021.

Diane Frank is author of seven books of poems, two novels, and a photo memoir of her 400 mile trek in the Nepal Himalayas. *Blackberries in the Dream House* won the Chelson Award for Fiction and was nominated for the Pulitzer Prize. She teaches at SF State and Dominican University.

Diana Glassman grew up in NYC. She has been writing since she was 14. She is a retired Social Worker and Acupuncturist and lives with her wife and their cat in Sebastopol. Since retiring, she has returned to her old passions of writing, singing, acting and traveling.
Music is Sheridan Gold's prayer and her poem. This retired Special Education and music educator is a Ner Shalom Good Shabbos Band member, tutors kids in academics, and teaches Silver and Native American Flute and hand drumming. She lives with her wife of 43 years and their many animals.

Dianna L. Grayer, Ph.D, is a multi-talented woman with vision. She is a Marriage and Family Therapist in private practice for over 25 years. Dianna loves empowering people and helping them become authentic. She's an author, workshop facilitator, playwright and director. For fun she enjoys nature, and Pinochle.

A Bronx-born daughter of German Jewish refugees, Basha Hirschfeld grew up in the beatnik era, later became a hippie, and then a radical feminist, leading protests and making films about change. Aside from the mundane miracles of motherhood and marriage, she has been a spiritual seeker all her life.

Myrna Joy was born in London, England in 1938. She emigrated to the US in 1961. She started writing poetry in 1982. She now lives in Sonoma County.

Anna Belle Kaufman is an artist and retired art psychotherapist. Her poetry and essays have appeared in *The Sun, Calyx, The Utne Reader, The Networker,* and *Brain, Child.*

Rabbi Irwin Keller has served Congregation Ner Shalom, Cotati, California as its spiritual leader since 2008. A former lawyer, LGBTQ and HIV activist, and performer, he received his ordination through the ALEPH Alliance for Jewish Renewal, in the lineage of Rabbi Zalman Schachter-Shalomi. His blog, Itzik's Well, is at irwinkeller.com.

Rita S. Losch: A life in 50 words? (5 so far, 42 to go.) Poet. Jew. Babyboomer. Lesbian. Sit-down comic. Maplewood. New Brunswick. San Francisco. Santa Rosa. Douglass College (BA English & Studio Art). SUNY-Stony Brook (MA English). Mills College (MFA Creative Writing). (Now we have reached 47 words. This makes 50.)

Barbara Lesch McCaffry, Ph.D., explores and untangles the work of contemporary feminist writers and poets (and also writes poetry). A Professor Emerita in Sonoma State University's Hutchins School of Liberal Studies, she is also involved in Holocaust and genocide education and coordinates Ner Shalom's *Beit Midrash*: Lifelong Jewish Learning program.

Margo Miller, a retired Jewish educator from an observant home, attended Yeshiva for three years and high school in Israel. Her Jewish practice in prayer, ritual, and text studies ground her teaching, continuing studies, and poetry. The poems included in this volume represent her first published work outside of academia.

Susan L. Miller has been writing for many years. From Rochester, NY, she attended college and nursing school in Israel and completed her nursing and studies in creative writing at Sonoma State University. She retired as a Public Health Nurse and has a Jin Shin Jyutsu practice.

Cyndi Norwitz has had various short pieces published or performed over the years, including Storahtelling and prayers for Congregation Ner Shalom. Her most recent publication is a Passover-themed comic for the anthology, *Why Faith?* She is working on a children's fantasy novel about the Exodus.

Linda Pantoskey, San Francisco Bay Area native, has resided among the pines of the Sierras as well as the redwoods of Marin, traveled widely, and now teaches part-time in Sonoma County. Linda, currently in Petaluma, CA, is blessed with three wonderful children, an amazing dog, and a very good life.

Nancy E. Rapp, a retired Marin County librarian and volunteer at the Museum of the American Indian, is a mixed-media artist and caretaker of the Congregation Ner Shalom Library. She has published essays and poetry in the *Modern Utopian, Left Coast Writer's 'Road Work,'* and the *Marin Independent Journal.*

Rita Rowan, a former Venezualan Peace Corps volunteer and Humanities teacher, lives in Santa Rosa with her husband, Terry, and dog Max. Her interest in poetry began when her father played Dylan Thomas recordings for her when she was a child.

Terry Rowan, a retired entrepreneur and educator, is the author of five books with another due for publication in the Spring of 2020, Terry is a husband, father of six children, and grandfather.

Adam Shemper is a psychotherapist in private practice in Healdsburg, California. He's also a photographer and writer—his images and words have appeared in *The New York Times, Los Angeles Times, San Francisco Chronicle, Time, MotherJones, The Oxford American, Shambhala Sun* and *Salon.com* as well as other publications.

Dafna Jo Simon is deeply committed to Judaism and her quirky family. She is courageous, a mother of four, married for 36 years, advocate for people with disabilities, avid reader, writer and musician, enchanted by animals and children. Dafna is an enthusiastic member of Congregation Ner Shalom.

Phil Temko was a professor of English, Humanities and Philosophy at Sonoma State University. He wrote 'things' on paper all his writing life. He engaged in solving difficult civil rights and liberties problems. He enjoyed music, books, and the great outdoors, especially the Oregon coast. He died December 19, 2019.

Lorenzo Valensi, a retired professional photographer, videographer, and producer of TV shows, commercials and industrial films, enjoys taking photos of nature around his country home. Find them on Facebook and #birdphotos. A musician and composer, his music for Ner Shalom can be found on the Ner Shalom site and YouTube.

Previous Publications

Grateful acknowledgement is made to the following authors for permission to reprint these works:

Alexandra Ellen Appel, "Hope" first appeared in *Burials*, 2003. "Remains" first appeared in *Roadside Markers*, 2012, and "For Our Children" first appeared in *Eagle Rock Poems*, 1996. Reprinted by permission of the author.

Abby Lynn Bogomolny, "The Lighted Pull of Dreams" first appeared in *Black of Moonlit Sea*, Herbooks, 1991. Reprinted by permission of the author.

Anna Belle Kaufman, "Cold Solace" first appeared in *The Sun*, 2012. Reprinted by permission of the author.

Acknowledgements

We extend our special thanks to these people and institutions without which this book would never have been written:

We are grateful to Reconstructing Judaism for their loving support of this congregation.

And we are grateful to ALEPH: Alliance for Jewish Renewal, whose inspiration has helped Ner Shalom become fertile ground for innovation, creativity and transcendence.

Irwin Keller - Our beloved Rabbi and guide who said one day, "Maybe it's time for us to have a book of poetry," then supported this project enthusiastically and creatively.

Ner Shalom Poets and Photographers - We are indebted to and blessed by our extraordinarily talented community of creatives from whom we were inspired to collect poems. We thought we might get a dozen contributors. To our amazement and delight we received beautiful poetry from 23 poets.

Bayit: Building Jewish and Rabbi Rachel Barenblat - we are grateful for Rabbi Barenblat's kindness, generosity and leadership, and help in concretizing our vision into reality. We are beyond grateful to be able to publish our work through Bayit.

Suzanne Shanbaum and Amy Gray - we wish to thank both Suzanne, the president of Congregation Ner Shalom at the time of writing, and Amy, president at the time of publishing, for their support and clear thinking.

We are grateful to Lorenzo Valensi and Adam Shemper
for their black and white images, Leiah Bowden for her
black and white images and her cover painting, Irwin
Keller for sharing his family's archived seder
photograph, and Doron Hovav for his critical eye.

Co-editors Abby Lynn Bogomolny, Sally Churgel and Rita
Rowan wish to thank Leiah Bowden; none of this would
have been possible without Leiah's conception of the book,
her diligence and dedication to carrying the torch with all
the niggling details and prodigious amount of work.

Our work together as an editorial team has been like a
poem that flows without effort or judgment but finds itself
on the page leaving the writer to wonder who truly is the
author.

Other Bayit Publications

Beside Still Waters: A Journey of Comfort and Renewal (with Ben Yehuda Press). This volume for the mourner's path contains liturgy and poetry for before death as well as for the stages of mourning and times of remembrance.

Color the Omer, Shari Berkowitz and Steve Silbert. This contemplative coloring book offers an artistic activity for each day of the journey from Pesach to Shavuot, along with short teachings designed to spark one's own revelation.

From Narrow Places: Liturgy, Poetry, and Art of the Pandemic Era, ed. Barenblat. This volume collects poetry, liturgy, and art co-created by Bayit's Liturgical Arts Working Group — a pluralist group of rabbis, liturgists, and artists — during the first eighteen months of COVID-19.

Renew Our Hearts: A Siddur for Shabbat Day (with Ben Yehuda Press.) Featuring liturgy for morning, afternoon, and evening along with curated works of poetry, art and new liturgies from across the breadth of Jewish spiritual life.

Find us online at yourbayit.org.

www.ingramcontent.com/pod-product-compliance
Lightning Source LLC
Chambersburg PA
CBHW020204090426
42734CB00008B/933